INTRODUCTION

In junior high school home economics class, we would take one-fourth yard of a fabric, and twist, and sew it to form a bias scarf as in the Bishop Method. Jane Hill of Hillcraft Needle Arts uses this as a base for Spiral Patchwork. It is the technique which was the inspiration for Spiraling.

While playing with strips of fabric to create new designs in strip piecing, I discovered that there are so many ways to treat this technique. Different fabric textures, colors, and combinations change the final appearance.

Establish a new approach to this old technique. Slice and dice the fabric; sew or serge it back together; then twist and sew again. This is an easy concept to create what looks like an involved procedure. *Spiraling Schemes and Chromatics* is designed as a guide for quick piecing and for using color to create wonderful wearables with an artistic approach.

As always, there are leftovers for other creations. Make a pillow. Add a matching handbag and belt to complete an ensemble. Treat leftovers in the sewing room like leftovers in the kitchen. Add a little something to create something new.

Keep on sewing and enjoy the many products that make it so much fun today!

CONTENTS

DICTIONARY FOR SPIRALING 2

CHOOSING THE FABRIC 3

CUTTING THE STRIPS 4

SEWING THE SETS 7

TO MATCH OR NOT TO MATCH 11

THE FINISHING TOUCH WITH...

    •*PIPING* 17

    •*CORDED PIPING* 18

    •*EMBROIDERED BEADING* 19

FOR ADDED LENGTH 20

PUTTING IT ALL TOGETHER 21

UNEVEN EDGE 22

3-D APPLIQUÉ 26

ESTIMATING THE YARDAGE 28

 DICTIONARY FOR SPIRALING

CORDED PIPING: A narrow fold of fabric filled with cord used for trimming seams to add dimension

CUTTING MAT: The cutting surface necessary when using a rotary cutter to avoid marring a table and injuring the blade

EMBROIDERY BEADING: A hemstitch with slits, through which ribbons can be laced

FILLER: The predominant color of fabric used repeatedly in a set. The fabric used to fill in and complete the set

PIPING: A narrow fold of fabric for trimming seams

 As in any venture, there are many tips and tricks which make sewing more efficient. These hints of special interest are designated with this symbol to emphasize information, speed sewing time, and create professional results

PRESSURE FOOT: That portion of the sewing machine which guards the needle and rests on the feet dogs causing the machine to feed the fabric. There are a wide variety of pressure feet available for various types of sewing. The techniques described with spiraling are easier to accomplish with the ¼" foot, the edgestitching foot, and the corded piping foot. For additional embellishment use the multi-cord couching foot and open toe appliqué foot

ROTARY CUTTER: A cutting device with a round blade attached to a handle resembling a pastry cutter designed to cut fabric

RULER: A see-through measuring tool with a straight edge and markings usually in ¼" increments. The most practical ruler for spiraling is 3" to 6" wide and 18" to 24" long. My favorite ruler is 3" by 18"

SET: Group of strips sewn together, usually 7" to 15" wide, intended for spiral piecing

SPIRALING: Winding upward from a center like the thread of a screw. Spiraling makes it simple to form larger bias strips from many narrow strips when a larger piece is desired. This very efficient technique simplifies the piecing with minimal fabric and time waste. Though the process begins with the same procedure, the outcome will vary drastically whether the sets are identical or varied, matched or unmatched

STASH: Acquiring, saving, stowing, and hoarding of fabrics, threads, trims, sewing equipment for leisure and necessary sewing

STITCH AND FLIP: Assembling technique used to combine strips of fabric on a base like muslin or batting whereby each added strip is sewn on the base and flipped before an additional strip is added

CHOOSING THE FABRIC

Various fabrics may be used for spiraling. The cotton weights for quilt making are easy to find, and the collection of color is enormous. Shop at quilt stores where the selection may be calico to very modern prints, plaids, and stripes. Many fabrics have a lamé print for extra focus.

The concept to remember most when selecting fabric is that the fabric does not need to match perfectly. Contrast in color, as well as sizes of print, makes a very effective design. Even a color that you would not use in a large piece can be used successfully in very narrow strips. The contrast you will get will cause the colors to bounce and compliment each other.

True, but very difficult to believe sometimes, is the fact that the fabric is going to be cut up, rather than used in a large full piece. If you come from a garment sewing background where the suit or skirt fabric was to match the blouse fabric perfectly, it will require deliberation for perfect coordination. Piecing requires the fabrics to be slightly off in various combinations for the design to work.

Purchase **one** yard pieces of fabrics when selecting colors to add to the stash. When a fabric is most desirable for the stockpile, more yardage may be necessary. Remember, this piece of fabric may enter into several projects during its lifetime. If the colors are a favorite, that combination will appear again. Purchase the fabric when you find it as the fabric may not be there on a future trip to the store.

On a recent teaching trip, I discovered a wonderful piece of fabric in the shop. Rather than put the piece aside to purchase immediately, I waited until packing my suitcases to begin my purchases. Discovering that my bolt was missing, I inquired with the salesperson. She had sold "my fabric" to one of the students in class. Of course the salesperson was unaware that I wanted the fabric. But she did quote me from class, "Remember, you said to get it while you can, even if you don't know what you want to do with it because it may not be there the next time you go to the store!" Sometimes we have to eat our words.

Because the full width of fabric is cut for this technique, my preference is to use fabric from the bolt rather than fat quarters or other smaller amount of fabric. Many times those small portions of fabric are just enough to frustrate me when I go to the cutting mat. So consider this when choosing fabric. It is always nicer to have a little extra, than to force creations from a limited supply of fabric.

Besides cottons, many other fabrics work nicely in spiraling. Lamé, whether knit or woven, (interface first for added strength and stability,) lightweight silks like dupioni or raw silk, wool or rayon challis, sandwashed rayon or silk, moiré taffeta, polyester or silk jacquards, velvet or velveteen are excellent choices. The combinations are endless.

The variety of fabrics available today make it fun to create a masterpiece of mixed texture with textiles. The interpretation of combinations becomes a creation of the creator. They are design choices.

CUTTING THE STRIPS

With modern conveniences like the rotary cutter, it is easy to cut many strips in little time. Rather than cutting one layer of fabric at a time, fold the fabric selvage to selvage across grain. This means all strips will be 45" long (width of fabric). Be certain fabric is not twisted in any way, but flat from the fold to the two selvages. The selvages should be perfectly even.

Fold the folded edge to the two selvages being careful to avoid any twists or wrinkles in the fabric *(Photo 1)*. Regardless of how the fabric was cut at the store, be certain the fabric is flat from folded edge to selvage. Sometimes fabric may be off grain. It may be impossible to straighten the fabric. Consequently, straight strips are more important than straight grain.

Use a rotary cutter, cutting mat, and see-through ruler at least three inches wide to straighten the fabric and cut the strips. Accuracy is important in the cutting. Use the ruler as a guide rather than guessing.

Align a right angle marking on the ruler with the folded edge of the fabric. With one hand on the rotary cutter, the blade next to the ruler, and the other hand on the ruler to hold it in position, straighten the uneven edges of the fabric *(Photo 2)*.

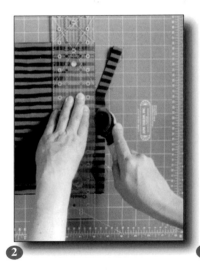

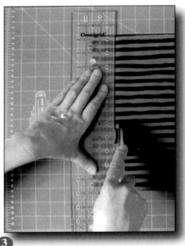

Turn the fabric around and position the ruler on the fabric so that an increment of the ruler is even with the previously cut edge. Using a sharp blade, cut the strip with one stroke *(Photo 3)*. A sawing motion as well as a nicked or dull blade will cause jagged edges. A clean finish, straight edge is most desirable.

Mixed widths from ¾" to 3" or 4" make an effective design. Most quilting rulers have ¼" marking. Use them as a guide for varying widths of strips. It is not necessary to make all strips identical in width. Allow ¼" on each side of the strip for seam allowances. Therefore, the width of the finished sewn strip is ½" narrower than the cut strip. A ¾" cut strip will leave ¼" visible.

Cut some strips ¾" when a minimal amount of that color is desired. Cut other strips 1", 1¼", 1½", 1¾", 2", 2½" and so on depending upon the design in the fabric or the amount of color desired. The narrower the strips are cut, the more strips are necessary to complete the project.

POINT OF INTEREST

•*Folding the fabric improperly will cause the cut strip to look like this (Photo 4).*

•*Fasten little pieces of fine sandpaper with double stick tape to the ruler to prevent sliding while cutting.*

•*Allow ¼" on each side of the cut strip for seam allowances.*

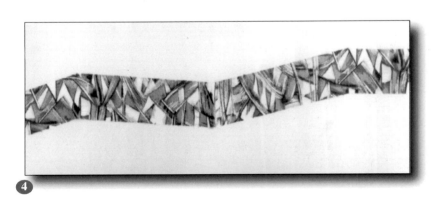

Divide a garment into sections with portions of spiraling and other areas of appliqué. *The Woven Vest #995*

The spiral workmanship is hidden in fabrics with similar background colors. Add embroidered beading with ribbon to add detail and contrast.

The easiest, most effective place to use matched spiraling is small areas of a garment like the shoulder or across the waist. *Linda's Vest #693*

Rather than make button holes, use a double row of buttons connected with small handbag chain.

Embroidered beading with gold edge trim ribbon add contrast to the predominant dark fabric. Purchased corded piping adds detail in the shoulder area and down the center front.
Saunter Satchel #901

Narrow piping adds the detail in the shoulder area.

Predominant green and gold with very little purple were spiraled in the upper portion. Mostly shades of purple were spiraled for the extension in the tunic length vest.
Shirt Tail Vest #595

SEWING THE SETS

Lay the strips on a surface in a sequence which is pleasing to the eye *(Photo 1)*. There are no set rules to follow. Use the color pages in this booklet as a guide to begin. Keep some strips close to the same width, while others may be wide combined with narrow. Use a very wide piece as a filler so the design is not so busy. Occasionally use a very bright or contrast fabric in a narrow strip. Consider light, medium, and dark fabric combinations. The types of prints as opposed to solid color combinations add variation. The most effective designs in the spiraling use many combinations of sets which **Do Not Match**. Be certain the strips on the outside edges look good next to each other. They will be stitched together in the spiraling process.

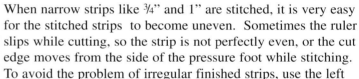

Though every machine on the market has a ¼" foot *(Photo 2)* for piecing, it is not necessary to use that foot in strip piecing. The most desirable width of seam allowance is ¼"; however, I sometimes change my mind and wish I had cut a strip narrower or slightly wider. Sewing with the basic foot *(Photo 3)* allows the freedom to move the needle position to the left or right to accommodate slight changes in width of fabric. Using the ¼" foot does not allow needle movement from center position. Any change will cause needle breakage. Experiment and use the foot which is most convenient.

When narrow strips like ¾" and 1" are stitched, it is very easy for the stitched strips to become uneven. Sometimes the ruler slips while cutting, so the strip is not perfectly even, or the cut edge moves from the side of the pressure foot while stitching. To avoid the problem of irregular finished strips, use the left side of the pressure foot as a guide and move the needle position to the desired width from the left. Position the presser foot next to the previously stitched row *(Photo 4)*. Leaning the presser foot against the ridge from the former row, stitch the new seam. It does not matter if the seam allowance is perfectly even. The important thing is that the visible strip of fabric is straight and uniform.

POINT OF INTEREST

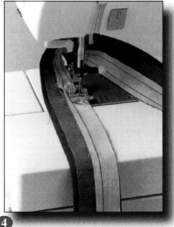

• *Use an 80 needle on cotton weight fabric.*

• *The life of a needle is about 8 sewing hours. Change needles as necessary.*

• *Choose a basic color thread which will work with all colors in the project like beige, gray, black, or navy. Always use the color close to the lightest strip in the project.*

• *The thread should correspond to the weight of the fabric used. Generally, my favorite thread is the Metrosene Plus polyester thread. There may be instances where 100% cotton sewing thread or 100% fine cotton embroidery (60 weight) thread works better.*

• *Fill several bobbins before starting a project. As one runs out, reload case and continue sewing. There is no need to pull the project away from the machine.*

• *Use a smaller stitch length like 2.0.*

• *Be certain the strips on the outside edges look good next to each other.*

5

Position the strips of one set to the left of the machine. Sew strips together in pairs using a 2.0 stitch length with the narrow strip on top or up. Continue from one pair to another without trimming the threads *(Photo 5)*. This will also keep the pairs in sequence. There is no need to back stitch. The smaller stitch length, combined with overlapping seams, prevents stitching from pulling out.

Press the seams together first to bury the stitches in the fabric *(Photo 6)*. Then press both seam allowances toward the darker fabric *(Photo 7)*.

Continue in the pairs process until the set is complete. Though it may seem practical to sew all strips together before pressing, the finished appearance is far more precise by sewing in pairs. Fewer extra tucks form in the pressing process.

The long strips stitched together or set should be at least 7" to 16" wide for the spiraling to work easily. Each set need not be exactly the same width. The wider the set, the easier it is to continue with the spiraling procedure on the sewing machine. There is no need to have a set wider than 16 inches!

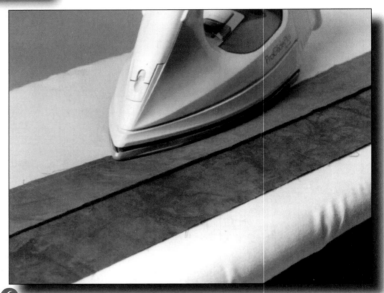

6

8

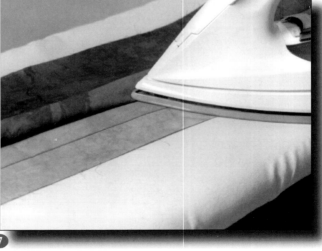

7

Using a see-through ruler and a rotary cutter, square both ends of the strip *(Photo 8)*. Accuracy is important. Beginning with a right angle makes future steps more precise. A crooked edge and seam cause future seams to be off slightly.

With the sewn strips *(Photo 9)* lying flat on a surface, fold one corner over to the side to form a bias angle. Folding some strips to the right and others to the left add variety to the finished project. When all strips are folded in the same direction, the diagonal is the same direction. By placing some folds to the right and others to the left, mirror images form *(Photo 10)*.

POINT OF
INTEREST

• *Sew with the narrow strip up or next to the pressure foot.*

• *Always press a seam before adding another strip to prevent little tucks from forming.*

Place pin in the ¼" seam at the corner *(Photo 11)*. Pivot the corner to align the longer, straight edges *(Photo 12)*. This may seem awkward at first, but it will work.

Start sewing the outer strips together *(Photo 13)*, forming a spiraling effect until reaching the end of the strip. This step forms a tube with pointed edges extending from both ends *(Photo 14)*.

When the seam is complete, make a press line along one side of the folded tube. Cut the fold off *(Photo 15)* with a ruler and rotary cutter to expose a larger piece of bias/diagonal parallel strips.

Cut strips of these diagonal pieces *(Photo 16)* remembering that $\frac{1}{4}$" seams from each side are removed in the finished piece. As in cutting the original strips, various widths of strips create a unique design. No set size of strips is required for spiraling in the pattern shown here.

Therefore, cut several strips in different widths and experiment with them to create a design. **Never** cut the whole set until design decisions are made. This allows the opportunity to change your mind and cut wider or narrower strips. Remember that strip piecing offers the opportunity to create as you go. Sometimes the outcome is a total surprise from the original plan.

Progressing through the book are some designs with definite cut widths or distinct schemes. Choose the idea which most suits the fabrics in your project. Or experiment to create a new arrangement.

To Match or Not to Match

1

Spiraling can offer a variety of opportunities–solid or figured fabrics, wide or narrow strips, gradation combinations rather than contrast. The easiest design is to use a variety of sets with *none* matching. The overall appearance is quite nice, appearing as though much more effort was involved than actually is.

To match the sets requires a slightly different approach and a completely different finish. Make *two* identical sets. The strips must be cut precisely the same width. It is preferable that the sewing is completed on one machine with seams sewn at the same seam allowance. Because one minor change can prevent the finished piece from matching, it is important to cut and sew precisely. The ends should be squared exactly alike.

Accuracy is of utmost importance! To form a mirror image, place the fabric strips as shown on page 9 *(Photo 10)*. Place a pin in the corner, pivot, and sew the strips together as described. Lay the stitched tubes next to each other making sure each tube spirals in a different direction.

Once the tubes of each set are cut open, it is easy to see how strips cut from the different sets will make a perfect match *(Photo 1)*. For an even zig zag finish, cut strips the same width from each set. When a hills and valleys appearance is desired, cut strips from one set narrow while strips from the other set are cut wider. Also consider making an extra set of the wider grouping.

To construct a vest with all matching sets, begin with *six* identical sets. Remember that each set must be matching. If a coat is preferred or a larger size is desired, begin with *eight* or more sets. These sets should be at least 12" wide.

If the strips do not match once the tubes are stitched and opened, do not worry. The solution is to become a little more creative *(Photo 2)*. Embroidery beading, corded piping, or other trim may be added between the seams to give the illusion of a matched seam *(Photo 3)*. Make each seam slightly off to add another designer touch *(Photo 4)*. Who is to judge the original intent?

2

The brainstorm occurred to me that I could make *six* identical sets into tubes. Once the tubes were open, I would cut *three* groups very narrow (1" to 2") and the other *three* groups much wider (3" to 4"). In the assembling stage, each wide strip would be placed between *two* narrow strips resulting in the hills and valleys appearance. As I began to sew these spiraled sets together, it was obvious that the sets would never match because one strip of one set was slightly narrower than the others. Rather than

ripping or inserting something, I chose to sew each strip slightly off to give the illusion of a new design. Sometimes designer touches just happen!

It is extremely important that all strips be cut at the same time with the same ruler. The strips should all be sewn on the same machine. You know you will be interrupted as you are sewing. You should have a plan to return to the same tool to complete the project. Otherwise, it will be very difficult to make the sets match in the finished project.

It may seem insignificant to change a tool, needle position, or machine, but any change may require a correction to make the match.

The easiest, most effective place to use matched spiraling is small areas of a garment like the shoulder or across the waist as on page 5. Otherwise use the unmatched or varied arrangement.

POINT OF INTEREST

• *Cut all strips with the same ruler.*

• *Sew each set with the same pressure foot on the same machine.*

• *If the needle position has been changed, make a note. All strips should be sewn at the same time.*

• *Because of the amount of strips and sets necessary for a large project, sew the pairs of all sets together at once, rather than sewing each set together individually.*

The *Cosmetic, Clutch and Tote #851* is versatile with spiraling on the diagonal.

Pink corded piping adds detail to spiraling on the *Portfolio #801*. The same pink fabric with piping and couched side panels completes the *Saunter Satchel #901*.

Embroidered beading allows variety and detail to pillows.

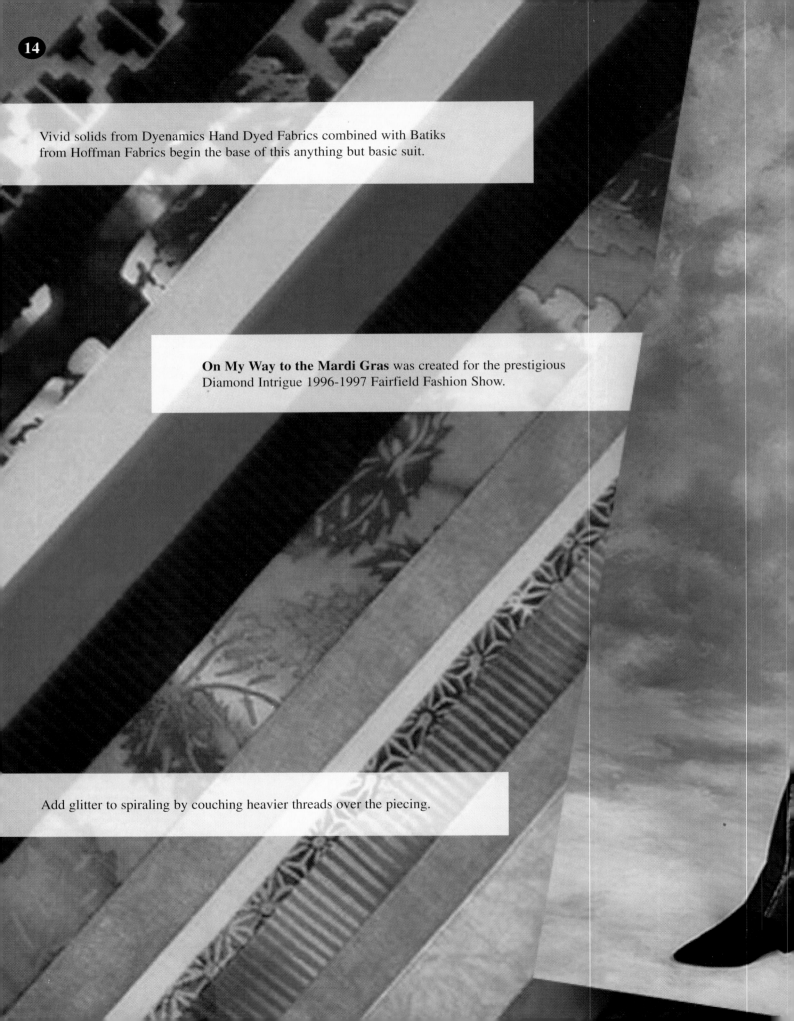

Vivid solids from Dyenamics Hand Dyed Fabrics combined with Batiks
from Hoffman Fabrics begin the base of this anything but basic suit.

On My Way to the Mardi Gras was created for the prestigious
Diamond Intrigue 1996-1997 Fairfield Fashion Show.

Add glitter to spiraling by couching heavier threads over the piecing.

Each year the Fairfield Show premieres at the Houston International Quilt Market, then travels to major quilt shows.

For 18 years the Fairfield Show has dazzled and entertained audiences with wearable art garments created by designers from around the world.

Color ribbon adds detail to the shoulder area. Black ribbon tones down the coloring in the hip area.

Add spiral length to the duster with black and polished black.
Shirt Tail Vest #595

Purple fills in the length on the tunic version.
Shirt Tail Vest #595

THE FINISHING TOUCH WITH...

To transform a garment into a fashion statement rather than just a spiraled vest, consider several elements. My preference is to add dimension and definition to the vertical seams. Sometimes, this addition is the complete length of the seam while others may cover a portion of the seam. Preference is determined by the finished design desired.

The ideas for this chapter are embroidered beading, piping, corded piping, and purchased decorative piping *(Photo 1)*.

Piping

Piping is simply a narrow strip of folded fabric inserted into a seam with a small edge remaining visible. Normally, this strip of fabric should be cut on the bias to accommodate curves and corners. However, because the placement on the spiraled garment is always straight, I sometimes cheat and cut my pieces crosswise on the fabric. The crosswise grain has a slight stretch making it the preferred choice for piping, rather than the length grain. When a stripe or plaid is used, always cut on the bias.

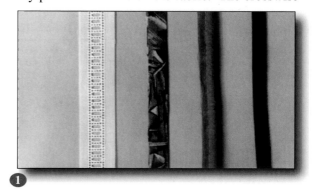

For piping, cut strips 1" wide. Fold and press the strips wrong sides together making the strip ½". Place the cut edge of piping even with the cut edge of the spiraled strip. Apply the

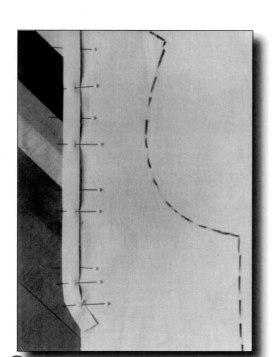

next strip right sides together encasing the piping between the two layers of strips. When using ¼" seam allowance, the piping is exposed ¼" when the strips are turned. If a slightly wider or narrower piece of piping is preferred, change the needle position from left or right to accommodate the desired finished width of piping. It does not matter if the seam allowance is generous or a skimpy ¼" as long as the raw edge is secure.

Rather than continue the piping the full length of the garment, consider using piping a partial distance. One of the best guidelines is to incorporate the piping in an area similar to the area of a yoke.

To finish the piping in a yoke area, curve the piping into the seam allowance at the point where the end is desired *(Photo 2)*. After stitching the seam, trim the excess piping. All rows of piping need not end at the same level of the garment. Actually, the best finish is obviously different levels.

Point of Interest

•*For a wider piping vary the width of the cut strip. Consider the position on the garment to avoid making the strip too wide.*

•*Consider the crosswise grain to save fabric for piping trim in straight areas.*

CORDED PIPING _____

Corded piping is a narrow strip of bias fabric containing a cord. Many times a purchased decorative corded piping is available to enhance the design. The purchased corded piping is available in basic fabric or decorative patterns by the yard or in small packages. However, other times none is available. So, make corded piping to match or with a contrasting fabric *(Photo 3)*. Traditionally, bias is used for corded piping. Always use bias with a stripe or plaid. However, because fabric gives on the crosswise grain, it is permissible to use the crosswise grain when trimming straight seams, like the vertical seams of spiraling.

Different sizes of cord will require different amounts of fabric. For small to medium corded piping the bias strips should be 1¼" wide. This technique is made easier by using one of the feet designed specifically for this purpose. Position the cording in the center of the strip of fabric. Fold the fabric in half over the cording and stitch with the cording or zipper foot. For very small cording, use the largest pintucking foot.

3

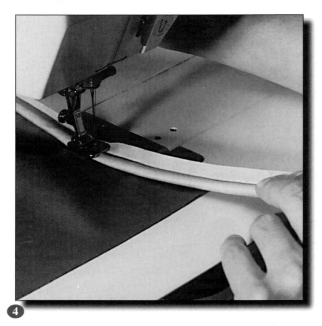

4

Keeping the cut edges together, place the cording under the ridge or tunnel in the foot *(Photo 4)*. Change the needle position to stitch close to the cording but do not stitch too close. When making corded piping, the bias fabric will be stitched three times eventually. Each stitching will be closer to the cording making the final stitching the closest. Moving the needle position for this purpose is ideal to avoid showing the previous rows of stitching.

Just as in the piping, the corded piping may not need to extend the full length of the garment. The corded piping will curve into the seam allowance just as the piping. Too much corded piping at the seam intersections will cause extra bulk. To eliminate the bulk, pull and trim the cording from the seam allowance where the corded piping curves into the seam allowance *(Photo 5)*. After trimming, run finger over corded piping to relax cord.

Point of Interest

•*Consider using several sizes of piping in one garment to add variety.*

•*Use corded piping only in the seams which cross the shoulder. It is not necessary to use corded piping in the seams under the arm.*

•*Use a double layer of fabric on coarsely twisted cording to prevent the ridges from showing through.*

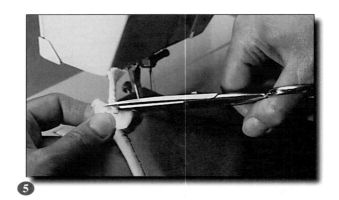

5

6

Another option in joining sections of spiraling, yet maintaining definition between the different rows of spiraling, is to use embroidered beading or faggoting. This type of beading is basically a batiste with embroidery stitching to form slits through which ribbon can be laced.

Normally the extra batiste on the edges of the beading is trimmed away. Align the edgestitching foot with the embroidery. Adjust the zig zag on the machine so that the zig goes into the hole of the embroidery and the zag goes over the edge *(Photo 6)*. In some instances, that is the proper way to use it.

7

However, to combine sections of spiraling that are bulky, this is the easiest and quickest method. This technique works best with straight seams because the width of the beading does not curve well.

With the beading on top, right sides together, match the cut edge of the batiste with the cut edge of the garment. Align the bar of the edge stitching foot *(Photo 7)* to the right ridge of the beading. This will act as a guide, making the stitching position accurate. Move the needle position to the right and stitch approximately 1/16" from the ridge. The small distance between the last ridge of the beading and the stitching allows the beading to turn. Known as the turn of the fabric, this technique helps maintain a flat seam. All the beading will be exposed and little bulk will remain in the seam allowance.

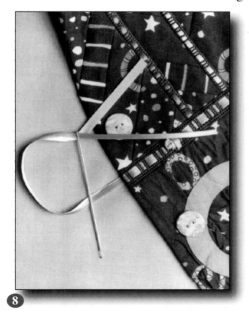

8

The original design for beading was to guide the ribbon evenly through the holes, weaving in a patterned manner. There is no rule that states that the weaving pattern must be symmetrical. If there is a rule, now is the time to break it! Guide the ribbon with a tapestry needle under some of the slits and over others. Do not establish a balanced design. Go over one, under three, over two, under five or what ever strikes your fancy. Remember, it is okay to break the rules. Every once in a while, tie a knot *(Photo 8)*. Allow the design and color of the ribbon to add dimension. Use two layers of ribbon through the same slits. When the knot is tied the colors will flip, making a two toned section. The variety of colors in the ribbon will add spark to the garment. Make a mistake once in a while. The mistake may lead to a better arrangement than the original plan!

•*Weave two ribbons through the slits of the embroidery rather than one. Tie a knot occasionally to change the color and add variety.*

•*Embroidered beading is available in white, ecru, and black. Use the spray on Tumble Dyes to add color.*

P OINT O F
I NTERES T

FOR ADDED LENGTH

There are length restrictions with a spiraled set. Generally, the cut strips begin with 45", the width of the fabric. Depending upon the length of the finished project, one set may not be long enough to complete a row on the project. Consider a tunic or full length garment. From a fashion point of view, repeating the same set may be too much repetitious color, too much of a certain design, or too much for a larger size.

Several options extend the length, making the garment a classic, more sophisticated piece rather than an overpowering clash of too much color and print. Consider the basic fabric used in the project. Is it a solid color or print? If it is a print, are the colors bolder or subdued? What is the overall feeling for the garment?

Sometimes it may be wise to add a solid color to the bottom of the garment, while other times it may be more appealing to add one of the darker printed fabrics. Make the garment pleasant to the eye. More attention should be drawn closer to the face, keeping the predominant colors and design in the shoulder and neck area. Corded piping or other trim in this area calls attention to the top of the garment. As the garment progresses towards the bottom, the design should darken, taking the viewing eye from the bottom of the garment to the top where most of the design is.

To use one fabric to extend the length of the garment, cut the added fabric at a 45° angle using the guidelines on a ruler. This is the same angle as the spiraled fabric *(Photo 1)*. Place right sides together with the point extended *(Photo 2)* so that the intersection of the two pieces is equal to the seam allowance. Stitch this seam and press towards the darker fabric *(Photo 3)*.

For other garments or projects, the overall appeal may need a continued spiral section. Make several additional spiraled sets with the darker colors from the upper sets or a new set of darker colors. These spiraled strips in the sets for the lower edge of a garment may be wider than the strips used in the upper portion of the garment.

Black cotton and black polished fabric create the illusion of two tones in the continuation of the *Pointillist Palette* fabric by Debra Lunn and Michael Mrowka for Robert Kaufman Co. on page 16.

Predominant green and gold with very little purple were spiraled in the upper portion of the Springs Industries, *I Heard It Through the Grapevine* by Ro Gregg. Mostly shades of purple were spiraled for the extension into the tunic length vest on page 6.

To add length to the Nancy Crow fabric by John Kaldor, embroidered beading with gold edge trim ribbon add variety in the upper portion of the garment while the darker groupings without the embroidery and gold were added to the bottom on page 6.

Continue the length of a garment according to the style and design of the garment. Choose a solid or figured darker fabric to fill in a small area. Continue a longer version with a spiraled piece. The options vary from garment to garment. Experiment, create, enjoy.

•The options for adding length are varied. Consider these ideas and the adventure for others begins to arise. One thing always leads to another.

POINT OF INTEREST

PUTTING IT ALL TOGETHER

B ecause the cut strips are on the bias, a foundation or base is necessary to maintain the shape of the garment. Several fabrics and battings are suitable for this project; however, the desired finished weight will determine which to use.

A light weight cotton, flannel, muslin, garment batting, or fabric from the stockpile which will never be used (make sure the color will not bleed or show through) make a good base and do not add too much to the weight of the garment.

Fairfield, Hobbs, Mountain Mist, Morning Glory, and Warm & Natural make a variety of battings which can be incorporated into a garment. The heavier or loftier batting may require a slightly larger size in the pattern to accommodate the extra bulk in the garment. Usually, going up half to one size is sufficient fabric to avoid making the garment too small.

Ghee's Shirt Tail Vest Pattern #595 is used to illustrate this technique, although any pattern could be used with this construction procedure.

This system is much like the quilt-as-you-go method or stitch and flip. Always cut the base larger than necessary for the finished project. With a removable marking pencil, mark the outline of the pattern directly on the base to use as a guide. When the base is a woven, be certain the outline of the pattern is on grain. Mark several other lines parallel to the grain at 2"– 3" intervals to assist in the stitching.

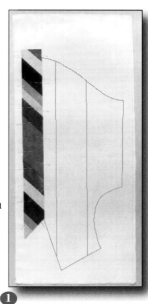
1

Generally it is advisable to begin in the center of a project and work outward. However, this may vary from project to project. On a garment back begin on the center back. On the front begin at the center front *(Photo 1)*, though the front has a cut edge and the back has a fold.

Place the first piece along a straight grain at the center, right side up. Pin at intervals with the pin perpendicular or right angle to the cut edge to hold the placement and prevent slippage. With right sides together place the second piece matching a cut edge *(Photo 2)*.

2

Open piece to expose right sides and continue in the same manner. Add the next piece, right sides together; stitch and open to expose the right sides. Because there is an outline guide on the base for the finished project, it is easy to judge where the next piece will be placed.

3

Continue to add pieces until the pattern shape markings drawn on the base are completely covered. Use the pattern as a guide to cut, rather than the drawn outline since it is possible for the base to shift with many seams. Baste ⅛" inside the marking *(Photo 3)*.

POINT OF INTEREST

•*Warmer climates need lighter backing, while cooler regions require heavier batting. Use the foundation suitable for the end use of the garment or project.*

UNEVEN EDGE

Variety is the spice of life. Sometimes, it is fun to complete a garment with an unusual finish. Why always have a straight or traditional lower edge? The shirt tail is a nice finish. But spiraling forms its own uneven edge. Why not let the bottom be determined by the design of the pieced garment?

Fully line the garment leaving the bottom edge completely open. The lining should be as long as the garment. Hang the garment from a hanger overnight to insure the fabric falls to a relaxed position. Pin the layers of piecing, backing, and lining together with pins vertical to the hem line. Using the desired finish color of thread in the bobbin as well as the top, stitch these layers together with a small straight stitch along the desired finished length. There should be at least 1/4" waste along the edge to avoid stretching the piecing *(Photo 1)*. This technique does not require a hem. The straight stitching will be the finished length. Nothing will be added and nothing taken away.

POINT OF INTEREST

•*Use the same color of thread in the bobbin as well as the top.*

•*A decorative thread like rayon or metallic makes an artistic finish.*

1

Match the same fabric as used in the herringbone to create an entirely different look.

Herringbone is easy to duplicate with spiraling. All strips are cut 1½ inches. All sets are cut 3½ inches. Offset each set as it is sewn together.
The Woven Vest #995

Create a tumbling block effect with a dark colored set between two light colored sets. The dark sets are cut 3½ inches wide with the narrow sets cut 2 inches wide.
Shirt Tail Vest #595

Spiraling forms its own uneven edge. Let the bottom of the garment continue the design in the spiraling. *The Woven Vest #995*

Dye the embroidered beading to match or add character to the garment.

Very carefully trim to this stitching. There should be no more than 1/16" fabric remaining between the stitching and the cut edge *(Photo 2)*. Use the point of the scissors to make clean, straight corners.

Zig zag over gimpe or a lightweight cord with a stitch width of 1-1/2 to 2 and length 1-1/2. The center hole of the multi-cord couching foot keeps the gimpe perfectly aligned. An open toe appliqué foot could be used for this purpose, however use caution to keep the cord straight and center *(Photo 3)*. The purpose of this stitching is to stabilize the finished edge with the gimpe to avoid stretching with wear. To use a satin stitch at this point causes a ripple. To make the prettiest finish requires stitching three times.

The final stitching is the most important. It covers the other stitching and gimpe, adds weight, and produces a rolled finished edge. Adjust the stitch width slightly wider than the previous zig zag to make certain the first stitching is covered. Adjust the stitch length to the perfect satin. This means the stitches lay side by side. Do not overlap or allow space between them. With the open toe appliqué foot stitch the final round over all previous stitches. The needle will go in the fabric to the left and into open air on the right causing the thread to overlap the edge with a smooth finish *(Photo 4)*.

It may be necessary to help the fabric along the corners since the feed dogs have nothing to hold to on the right side. Do not rush at this point. It takes time for the machine to complete the stitching. Do not push the fabric. If the rolled finish is not filled in sufficiently, make a fourth round. Be certain the stitch width is slightly wider than previously sewn.

POINT OF INTEREST

•*It may be necessary to tighten the tension slightly for smoother coverage.*

•*When a bit of the backing or fabric shows through the rolled stitching, use a permanent marker the color of the stitching to hide the undesirable.*

•*It requires time to complete the final stitching of the uneven edge. Go slow. It is worth the effort.*

3-D Appliqué

Spiraling makes a wonderful base for other embellishment. With the time involved to make the piecing, it is not practical to completely cover the spiraling. A portion of the garment or project could be enhanced with additional appliqué to draw attention to other areas of the garment.

Study fabrics in the stash or at the store. So many of the fabrics available today have large designs which could be pulled from the fabric and appliquéed to a pieced base. Impressions, by Pat Campbell and Michelle Jack for Benartex is the perfect selection for making 3-D appliqué. The tulips grace the front cover.

The designs should be relatively simple, without too much detail. Depending upon the position used in the project, the design should be proportionate so as not to overpower the project. The tulips used in the shirt tail vest on the cover and page 14 are roughly 3" wide by 4" long. The grape section is approximately 6" long by 5" deep. Different leaves were used to fill in the background. Choose designs which are in this size range. An appliqué which is too small may be difficult to stitch considering the detail.

It takes 3 of one design to make 1 dimensional appliqué. Be sure to examine the repeat in the fabric. A fabric which has a large repeat may not be practical to use with this process.

Choose the design desired for the project. Place a paper backed fusing medium on the wrong side of the fabric in the appliqué area following the manufacturer's instruction *(Photo 1)*. Remove the paper backing from the fabric after the fabric cools. Otherwise the fabric may stick to itself from the warm fusing medium.

Trim on the inside line of the appliqué. Straight stitching is used in this variety of appliqué. Therefore, any excess fabric on the trim line will be visible on the finished garment.

❶

Steam the appliqué in position on the garment. When making flowers apply the stems and leaves at this point. The next layer of flower appliqué will cover the ends of the stems.

For effect straight stitch around the appliqué twice starting and stopping in an area which will be covered by the next layer. Stitch other lines on the appliqué to add detail where desired *(Photo 2)*. Choose a decorative thread like rayon or metallic. Use the proper needle for the type thread chosen. A slightly longer stitch length like 2½ to 3 works best.

Place fusing medium on the other 2 appliqué portions. Trim one to the desired size using the outside of the design as a guide. Also trim away the background petals *(Photo 3)*. This means the upper layer of appliqué is slightly larger than the one fused to the garment.

To add dimension use a layer of lightweight batting between the layers of upper appliqué. It should be trimmed approximately ⅛" smaller around the entire appliqué. To avoid pressing onto the iron, fuse in position with the paper backing from the fusing medium or a Teflon sheet.

❷

Place this layer wrong side to wrong side on the third appliqué portion. Because the design is reversed it may not meet exactly. In this instance, be sure the area which is open in the final position is the same coloration as the majority of the appliqué.

Fuse these layers together with the Teflon sheet. Trim layers evenly around the appliqué. Stitch any detail lines along the open side and within the middle of the appliqué with decorative thread.

Position this upper layer of appliqué on top of the first layer fused to the garment. Since this upper layer is trimmed on the outside lines and the stitched appliqué is trimmed on the inside lines, the upper appliqué portion is slightly larger than the lower portion. Force the outer layer to match the lower level, making the upper portion 3-dimensional. Stitch around the outside edge to complete the appliqué *(Photo 4)*.

•*It requires 3 of one design to make 1-dimensional appliqué.*

•*Choose a design for appliqué in proportion to the garment.*

•*Use sharp pointed scissors to accurately cut appliqué.*

•*Remove paper backing from fused fabric after the fabric cools.*

•*Use an embroidery needle with rayon thread.*

•*Topstitch or Metafil needles work best with metallic thread.*

•*A Teflon sheet makes appliqué easier and avoids pressing design onto the iron.*

•*A slightly longer stitch length like 2½ to 3 works best for decorative thread in the 3-D appliqué.*

POINT OF INTEREST

ESTIMATING THE YARDAGE

Determining the amount of fabric can be very tricky. From my Scottish background, I am inclined to purchase the exact amount, sometimes cutting myself a little short. Therefore, I attempt to purchase more than ample to avoid unnecessary creative blunders, aches and pain. Most of the time I never know what I am going to do until I do it. It is permissible to have too much.

Originally, a yardage chart was planned to help you calculate yardage needed for different size projects. After constructing many samples, using a variety of fabrics, I find it impossible to give exact yardage for any projects. There are too many variables. I purchase fabrics differently for piecing projects, than for whole garments. My philosophy is to adapt basic techniques to the fabrics chosen for the project. When I considered that fabrics similar to the ones used in this book may not be available and all of the other variables, I abandoned my plan to give you a yardage chart. I know you will understand once you start cutting and sewing the sets.

The easiest calculation is to have the total of all yardage combined equal the necessary yardage to make that garment. For instance, if the garment requires 1½ yards to complete, and there are six fabrics used, ¼ yard is necessary of each fabric. The spark or filler color may require more fabric, while the other colors may require less. Some fabrics, perhaps leftovers from another project, may have 1 or 2 strips. This amount is hardly enough to consider in yardage. But, leftovers of several different strips begin to add up as the process continues. Piping, corded piping, tucks, and other detail procedures use fabric, too. It never hurts to have more fabric than necessary.

Consider the following guidelines to work with most sizes. Add another set or two for larger sizes.

- *Four sets 16 inches wide make a short length (just below the waistline) vest for most sizes front and back.*

- *Allow six sets with two of the sets in darker shades for tunic length.*

- *Allow eight sets with four of the sets in darker shades for duster length.*

- *Two narrow sets 10-12 inches wide make a partial garment front or one side of the garment on all sizes.*

- *A garment with the tumbling block method uses four darker and two lighter sets each 12 to 16 inches wide. Allow more sets for longer length.*

- *Herringbone spiraling uses equal amounts of two fabrics. One fabric could be a bold geometric print and the other fabric a solid.*

- *Spiraling a large print generally uses equal amounts of that print fabric and one solid color fabric.*

- *Purchase 2 yards of stripe or gradation fabrics. This allows 45 inches to cut lengthwise and ¾ yard to cut crosswise.*

Enjoy the adventure of spiraling!

Linda